Secret of Mahabharata

Meaning behind the epic war story

By
Sri Kutupananda Nath

Pondicherry , India
Karthik Purnima , Nov 2024
kutupanandanath@gmail.com

Few words

This book is channeled work . Idea , words , expressions in original 72 sanskrit verses came from beyond by blessings of Sage Vyasa , author of original Mahabharata , Puranas & Bhagvata . On the day of 20 April 2017 , these 72 sanskrit verses were channeled by me in Sangli , Maharashtra . It was Chaitra Krishna Ashtami Tithi & Shravan Nakshatra , which deity is Vishnu . Though I am good at Sanskrit , I am not expert in sanskrit grammer or poetry . I used to write poems in marathi in my child days & youth . But this sanskrit poetry is not mine . These verses are in anushtubh chhanda , one of the 7 Chhandas , metre in which Ramayana , Mahabharata , Puranas were written . These verses came in mind and I wrote them continuously in three hours . Day 20th April is also important . Occultist will know its importance as its birth day of one powerful personality .
I have immense respect to Sage Vyasa whom I had fortune to interact in dreams few times . In my last birth I was accomplishing his work from 1924 onwards . This birth though remains

mystery to me , his insights & dreams about him keep taking me to path further . And this is year 2024 , another synchronicity .
Mahabharata has four beginnings & four meanings viz Adi Parva,Astika Parva , Pauloma Parva , Uparichara Parva . These four beginnings are four layers in which parallel four interpretaions are waved together . Adi is start of total compilation of one lac verses .
Uparichara is surface meaning ie story of war over kingdom & rivalary between brothers . Deeper meanings are Astika & Pauloma . In them Astika meanings what actually was is actual meaning . These 72 verses gives secret of Astika meaning .
Sanskrit verses are channeled verses , english commentary & explaination is only mine

To
Sage Vyasa
and
To two Rishis , Ruru of Bhrigu Kula &
Astika of Naga Kula

Introduction

The Mahabharata, one of the greatest epics in human history, is a treasure trove of spiritual wisdom, moral dilemmas, and profound philosophical insights. Beyond its surface narrative of familial conflict and heroic exploits lies a deeper, esoteric layer of meanings and teachings. The Secret of the Mahabharata aims to uncover these hidden dimensions, offering readers a unique perspective on the epic that goes beyond traditional interpretations. The purpose of this book is to illuminate the profound secrets embedded within the Mahabharata, which have often remained obscured by the complexity of its narrative and the multiplicity of its commentaries. Through an in-depth analysis of selected verses, the book seeks to reveal the esoteric teachings and divine mysteries that Sage Vyasa, the author of the Mahabharata, subtly wove into the fabric of the epic. This exploration is intended to provide spiritual seekers, scholars, and enthusiasts with a richer understanding of the Mahabharata's true essence, guiding them towards greater wisdom and enlightenment.

The book is structured around 73 verses that encapsulate the core themes and hidden meanings of the Mahabharata. Each verse has been meticulously analyzed to uncover the layers of symbolic and metaphysical insights it contains. The verses cover a wide range of topics, including:

1.Divine Incarnations and Dharma :The verses discuss the various incarnations of the Supreme God in different forms and species, highlighting the role of divine intervention in establishing and maintaining dharma (righteousness) across epochs. For instance, the incarnations of Vishnu as a boar, lion, dwarf, and other forms emphasize the adaptive strategies of the divine to restore balance in the universe.

2.Cosmic Cycles and Evolution :The text delves into the cyclical nature of time and the ongoing battle between divine and demonic forces. The concepts of Yugas (ages), Manvantaras (epochs), and Kalpas (eons) are explored, illustrating the perpetual motion of the cosmic wheel and its impact on the evolution of consciousness.

3.Human Nature and Destiny : The Mahabharata's insights into human nature are profound, explaining how the interplay of the three Gunas (qualities: Satwa, Rajas, Tamas) and the four Varnas (social classes) shape individual destinies. The verses underscore the importance of understanding one's inherent nature (Swabhava) and performing actions (Karma) in alignment with it to achieve spiritual liberation.

4.Metaphysical Symbolism: Many verses employ metaphors and symbols to convey deeper truths. For example, the dice game between Duryodhana and Yudhishthira symbolizes the cosmic game of fate and destiny, where human actions are influenced by divine will. The characters themselves represent various cosmic principles and forces, making the Mahabharata a rich allegorical tapestry.

5. Spiritual Practices and Realization : The text emphasizes the importance of Karma Yoga (the yoga of action) and the transformative power of Yajna (sacrifice). It explains how performing actions without attachment to results, guided by divine consciousness, leads to spiritual elevation. The verses also highlight the role of divine possession in achieving true Karma Yoga, where the practitioner becomes an instrument of the divine will.

 Insights and Reflections

The Secret of the Mahabharata offers several key insights that can profoundly impact one's spiritual journey:
Interconnectedness of All Life : The Mahabharata portrays the intricate web of connections between all beings and the universe, emphasizing the unity of creation. Understanding this interconnectedness fosters a sense of compassion and responsibility towards all life forms.
Role of Divine Guidance :The epic illustrates the

importance of seeking and surrendering to divine guidance. Characters like Krishna and Vyasa serve as embodiments of divine wisdom, guiding humanity through the complexities of life and karma.
Transcendence of Dualities : The eternal struggle between Devas and Asuras, good and evil, is a central theme. The Mahabharata teaches that true wisdom lies in transcending these dualities and recognizing the underlying oneness of existence.
Evolution of Consciousness :The text underscores the dynamic nature of consciousness and its evolution through various forms and experiences. This perspective encourages personal growth and spiritual evolution as an ongoing, transformative process.
Eternal Relevance: The Mahabharata's teachings are timeless, offering guidance for contemporary issues and challenges. Its lessons on duty, righteousness, and the pursuit of truth remain relevant, providing a moral and spiritual compass for modern life.
The Secret of the Mahabharata invites readers to embark on a journey of discovery, delving into the profound mysteries and timeless wisdom of this ancient epic. By uncovering the hidden layers of meaning and exploring the esoteric dimensions of the text, this book seeks to enrich our understanding of the Mahabharata and its relevance to our spiritual and everyday lives. It is an invitation to look beyond the surface narrative and engage with the deeper truths that have inspired and guided humanity for millennia .

Secret of Mahabharata
महाभारत रहस्य

भारतेषु सहस्राणि भाष्या: सन्ति किम यत्नः |
अपि ते सन्ति बहवः राजते इदं गूढार्थदीपिका ||1||

There are many commentaries on the epic poem "Mahabharata," so what is the purpose of this new effort? Despite the large number of existing commentaries, this new commentary aims to shed light on the secrets of the "Mahabharata."

In ancient India, the "Mahabharata" was considered a significant text and was widely studied and analyzed. Despite the extensive commentary and interpretation that already exists, this new effort hopes to bring something unique to the table by uncovering hidden meanings and symbolism within the poem.

This new commentary intends to provide a deeper understanding of the "Mahabharata" by highlighting its intricate details and illuminating aspects of the story that may have been previously overlooked. It is a new contribution to the rich tradition of scholarship and interpretation surrounding this ancient text.

By shining a light on the secrets of the "Mahabharata," this commentary aims to deepen the

reader's appreciation for this epic poem and to
provide a new perspective on its timeless themes and
messages.

व्यासो भगवान् हरि विवासयत वेदाः सन् |
गीताशास्त्रं कृतवान मन्दबोधानाम् कलौ युगे ||2||

Lord Vishnu, in the form of Vyasa, extracted the
essence of the Vedas and composed the
"Mahabharata." The "Bhagavad Gita," a key text
within the "Mahabharata," is the very essence of the
epic poem.

Vyasa, a revered sage in Hindu mythology, was
believed to have been an incarnation of Lord Vishnu.
According to legend, he was tasked with bringing
order to the chaos of the Vedas, which were a
collection of sacred hymns and knowledge from
ancient India.

By distilling the essence of the Vedas and creating
the "Mahabharata," Vyasa aimed to provide a more
accessible and understandable interpretation of these
ancient texts. The "Bhagavad Gita," which is a central
part of the "Mahabharata," is considered a highly
influential text in Hindu philosophy and spirituality.

In composing the "Mahabharata," Vyasa sought to
provide a framework for understanding the complex
and multifaceted teachings of the Vedas. By doing so,
he created a text that has endured for thousands of

years and continues to be studied and revered by generations of followers.

वेदानां बहवः शाखा अवर्तयत पुरा |
व्यासः अकथयत अर्थानां उपबृंहणये ||3||

The Vedas are ancient Hindu scriptures that form the basis of Hinduism. They contain hymns, prayers, and rituals. The Vedas are considered to be the oldest scriptures in the world, and they have been passed down orally for generations. There were many versions of the Vedas that existed in ancient times.

Vyasa was a revered sage in Hindu mythology who is credited with authoring the Mahabharata and compiling the Vedas. According to Hindu tradition, Vyasa was asked to explain the meaning of the Vedas to the masses, as they were written in Sanskrit and were difficult to understand. To do this, Vyasa created a new version of the Vedas, known as the Bharata, which was written in a language that was easier to understand.

The Bharata was a simplified version of the Vedas that explained the meaning of the original scriptures in a way that was accessible to the masses. It was written in Sanskrit, but it used a simple, straightforward language that was easy for people to understand. Vyasa's goal was to make the Vedas more accessible to the general public, so that they could benefit from their teachings.

विनावीर्यराजनःस्त्रीभ्यः दत्तः बीजं मुनिः |
तत् खलु अभवत् वृक्षः भारतनाम्ना वेदः ||4||

The sage gave the seed to the queens of the impotent king.
From this seed, a great tree grew which bore the fruit of the Vedas.
This Vedic text was named Bharata after the king.
The text was then passed down through the generations, providing valuable insight into the ancient Hindu scriptures.
It is still widely studied and revered today for its rich tradition and timeless wisdom.

धृतराष्ट्रः नागो असुरः पण्डु : अबलः मनुष्यः |
पुत्रौ प्राप्तवन्तौ सापत्नौ यमः साक्षी सर्वस्य ||5||

Dhritarashtra was a serpentine king, while Pandu was a weak human.
Both of these kings were born to two different queens.
Along with them, Yama was born as Vidura, who was a witness to all that happened.
Vidura was known for his wisdom and fair judgment,

and he played a key role in the events that took place during his time.
He was highly respected for his honesty and impartiality, and his role in the story is still remembered and revered to this day.

कथा नैतत् युद्धस्य अस्ति खलु युगकथा |
चक्रस्य गतिः कालस्य देवासुराणां विभाग: ||6||

refers to a story that encompasses the entire eon, not just a single war. It is about the motion of time and the struggle between the Devas and Asuras. The use of the word "चक्रस्य गति:" (motion of time wheel) refers to the cyclical nature of time, where everything repeats itself in a continuous cycle. The conflict between the Devas and Asuras symbolizes the eternal battle between good and evil that occurs in every age.Expanding further, the struggle between the Devas and Asuras represents the constant tension between righteousness and unrighteousness. The Devas symbolize the forces of good and light, while the Asuras symbolize the forces of evil and darkness. The motion of the time wheel indicates that this struggle will continue to repeat itself in every age and that it is a never-ending cycle. The use of the word "युगकथा" (story of eon) emphasizes the importance of this struggle as it encompasses the entire timeline of creation.

प्रकृति: महाशक्तिः भुवने सर्व ग्रहे ग्रहे |

युगमन्वतरकल्पेषु क्रीडति द्यूतं महत् ||7||

refers to the highest power, Prakriti, that is present in all universes and planets. The use of the word "महाशक्तिः" (greatest power) emphasizes the importance and dominance of Prakriti. It is said that Prakriti plays the game of dice in every Yuga (age), Manu (cycle of creation) and Kalpa (time frame). Expanding further, the game of dice symbolizes the unpredictable nature of life and the ups and downs that come with it. The use of the word "क्रीडति" (plays) also indicates that this is not a forced or predetermined outcome, but rather a playful and natural occurrence. The game of dice encompasses all of creation, including the cycles of creation, preservation and destruction. The mention of Prakriti playing the game in every Yuga, Manu and Kalpa highlights the idea that this game is not limited to a single cycle, but occurs in all cycles of time. The use of the word "महत्" (great) indicates the significance and impact of this game on all of creation.

अक्षसुत्राणि असन्ख्यानि नवयोनिषु कर्मेभिः |
मानसप्राणभौतिकसृष्टयः प्रसवति सा ||8||

Dices roll in innumerable times in all nine species according to their karmas
Prakriti creates worlds of mind , vital and physical .
The first verse says that in all nine species (thought to be different categories of existence), dices (representing fate or destiny) roll countless times and

dictate the actions of individuals based on their karmas (actions or deeds in previous lives). The universe is governed by the laws of cause and effect, and individuals reap the consequences of their past actions in this life and future lives. Additionally, Prakriti (the divine feminine force responsible for the creation and evolution of the universe) creates the different worlds of the mind, vital, and physical.

मन्वन्तरे युगे युगे एके एके ग्रहे ग्रहे |
स्थावरजलनभभूमीषु चित्शक्ति प्रयच्छति ||9 ||

The second verse says that on different planets and during different eras, the power of consciousness enters into various forms such as land, water, sky, and earth. The verse is emphasizing that consciousness is not limited to the human form and permeates all of existence. The idea is that the universe is alive with consciousness, and that everything is interconnected and part of a larger cosmic consciousness.

पशूनां देवपर्यन्तं कालगति उत्सर्पिणि |
देवात् पशुत्वान्ते चित्नदि अवसर्पिणि ||10||

From animals to deities evolution takes place through time
From deities to animals involution takes place of consciousness It
says that evolution takes place over time, starting from animals and culminating in the form of deities. At

the same time, there is also involution, where consciousness moves from the level of deities to that of animals. The idea is that consciousness is constantly evolving and devolving, moving in cycles through various forms of existence.

वैवस्वतमन्वन्तरे अस्मिन् अष्टाविंशति कलौ |
अस्यां भूमौ भ्रमति कालचक्र: चित्शक्त्य: ||11||

In Vaivasvata manu and of 28th Kali yuga
On the island of Jambu , timewheel of consciousness rotates . It says that in the current era, the time-wheel of consciousness rotates on the island of Jambu during the 28th Kali Yuga in the reign of Vaivasvata Manu. The verse emphasizes that the evolution of consciousness is not a linear process but takes place in cycles, each cycle building on the lessons learned from previous ones.

रविबुधशुक्रेषु च सोमस्य लोके तथा |
आवर्तयत चक्रमेतत् भौमान्ते भविष्यति || 12 ||

From Sun , this evolution starts which goes in sequence of mercury
 Venus moon . It ends on Mars .
Further , this evolution of consciousness starts from the Sun and proceeds in a sequence through Mercury, Venus, the Moon, and ends on Mars. The verse is outlining the cosmogony of Hinduism and the different stages of consciousness that exist in the

universe. The idea is that the universe is constantly evolving, and that individual consciousness is a part of this larger process of cosmic evolution

नागपिशाचयक्षरक्षा:देवगन्धर्वाः अपि तथा |
वानरासुरैः ऋषिभिः सह मनुष्यान्ते पुर्नयति ||13 ||

Evolution cycle sequence is Nagas, Pishachas
Yakshas Rakshas Devas Gandharvas
Vanaras Asuras Rishis and ends in Manushyas

मनुष्याः खलु मानसपुत्रा: देवानां वरिष्ठाः |
नागेभ्यः मनुपर्यन्तं विकासयति चक्रं महत् ||14||

Manusyas are true mind born sons of Higher Gods
From Nagas till Manushyas this cycle evolves

धर्मसंस्थापनार्थाय जन्मिनः भगवान् सदा |
पशुवानरमनुष्येषु असुरगन्धर्वराक्षसेषु तथा || 15 ||

To establish law , Supreme God takes births in
animals monkeys humans
Asura gandharva rakshasa species

वराहनृसिंहपशुषु वामन: परशुधरः असुरेषु |
गन्धर्वेषु श्रीरामौ मत्स्यकुर्मौ जलचरौ पुरा ||16||

He took birth in animals as boar and lion . He born in
asuras(assyrians & persians) as Parashuraam
In gandharvas as Raam and as fish , tortoise in
aquarius species long back

The above verses describe the evolution cycle in Hindu mythology. According to the verses, the cycle starts with Nagas (a group of serpentine beings) and progresses through Pishachas (ghostly beings), Yakshas (supernatural beings), Rakshasas (demonic beings), Devas (gods), Gandharvas (heavenly musicians), Vanaras (a group of monkey-like beings), Asuras (demons), Rishis (sages), and finally ends in Manushyas (humans).

The verses explain that Manushyas are considered the true mind-born sons of the higher gods. The evolution cycle starts from Nagas and progresses till Manushyas, where the cycle evolves.

The verses also state that the supreme god takes births in various species, including animals, monkeys, and humans, in order to establish the law. He takes birth in different species, such as boars and lions as animals, Parashuram in Asuras, Raam in Gandharvas, and as a fish and tortoise in the aquatic species. All these births were taken to establish law and order.

In conclusion, these verses describe the evolution cycle in Hindu mythology and the role of the supreme god in establishing the law through his various births in different species.

भगवान प्रजापिता भुवनस्य गोप्ता |
भ्रामयति विश्वचक्रं देहारुढः स्वमायया ||17||

Lord creator knower of all universes moves this cycle
of world by taking different bodies with
Help of his own Maya shakti

सः कर्ता कर्माणां स भोक्ता फ़लानम् च |
यज्ञस्य यजमानोऽपि फ़लदातारः देवता ||18 ||

He is doer of Karmas and enjoyer of fruits of Karmas
He is doer of sacrifice , He is deity of effects

परित्राणाय सत्यजगते विनाशार्थे असतकृते |
युगान्ते कर्मयोगी सः जन्मयति बहुषु देहेषु ||19||

To protect the true world and end the dark material
one
At end of eon this yogi of karma takes births in many
bodies

एषः साक्षी भूतानां प्रेरको कर्माणां अपि |
एतस्मात् जायते सर्वं तत् सर्वं विनश्यति ||20||

He is witnesser of all souls , he incites their karmas
From him all is born , in him all dies

Commentary for above four verses
Verse 17: Lord Creator, known as Prajapati, governs
the cycle of the world by taking on different bodies
with the help of his own Maya Shakti.

The verse speaks about Lord Prajapati, who is the
creator and the knower of all universes. He is the one

who moves the cycle of the world by taking on different bodies. The process is enabled by his own Maya Shakti, which is a divine power that allows him to control the illusions and delusions in the world. This verse highlights the supreme power and control of Lord Prajapati over all universes and everything in them

Verse 18: He is the doer of actions and the enjoyer of the fruits of actions. He is the performer of sacrifices and the deity of the effects of sacrifices.

This verse emphasizes the dual roles of Lord Prajapati as both the doer and the enjoyer of actions. He is the one who performs actions and also reaps the fruits of those actions. He is also described as the performer of sacrifices and the deity who receives the effects of those sacrifices. This verse highlights the omniscient and omnipotent nature of Lord Prajapati and his control over all actions and their outcomes.

Verse 19: To protect the true world and end the dark material one, at the end of the eon, this yogi of karma takes births in many bodies.

This verse speaks about the purpose of Lord Prajapati taking on different bodies. He takes births in many bodies to protect the true world and end the dark material one. This is done at the end of an eon, which is a significant period in Hindu cosmology. Lord Prajapati is referred to as a yogi of karma, indicating that he is one who practices yoga to control his actions and attain spiritual liberation

Verse 20: He is the witnesser of all souls and incites their karmas. From him all is born, in him all dies.

The verse highlights the all-encompassing nature of Lord Prajapati. He is the witnesser of all souls and incites their karmas, meaning that he observes all actions and influences their outcome. He is also described as the source of all existence, as all is born from him, and in him all ultimately dies. This verse emphasizes the absolute power and control of Lord Prajapati over all things in the world.

कर्मयोगी सारथिः सन् महाभारतस्य द्रष्टा |
अर्जुनस्य गुरुः अपि दुर्योधनस्य सखा ||21||

He is a Karma Yogi, a charioteer, the seer of the Mahabharata, the guru of Arjuna, and yet also a friend of Duryodhana.
This verse highlights the multifaceted role of Lord Krishna in the "Mahabharata." As a Karma Yogi, Krishna represents the ideal of action without attachment, guiding the war's course with profound understanding yet without personal investment in its outcome. His role as Arjuna's guru signifies his role as a teacher who imparts the essence of Dharma (righteousness), while his friendship with Duryodhana shows his impartiality, as he treats each soul according to their unique path in the cosmic play. He

embodies the perfect balance between engagement and detachment, maintaining relationships with both the protagonists and antagonists, seeing each as integral to the unfolding of universal order.

Krishna's presence as both a teacher and friend to opposing forces demonstrates the neutrality of divine wisdom. He does not judge but offers guidance to those who seek it. By acting as a charioteer, he places himself in a role of servitude, symbolizing humility and the willingness to assist in the path of Dharma without attachment to outcomes. This duality —being a guide to Arjuna and a friend to Duryodhana —illustrates the transcendent nature of divinity, which operates beyond human dualities and embraces all paths in its grand play.

नकुलसहदेवौ अश्विनौ भीमार्जुनौ इन्द्रवायवौ |
शतनागाः कौरवाः च द्रौपदी: अयं पृथिवीः ||22||

Nakula and Sahadeva are the Ashwin twins; Bhima and Arjuna are embodiments of Indra and Vayu, respectively. The Kauravas are a hundred reptilian asuras, and Draupadi represents the earth.
This verse alludes to the symbolic identities of the Pandavas, each embodying divine archetypes. Nakula and Sahadeva represent the Ashwin twins, divine healers and bringers of light, signifying the

vitality and balance needed to uphold Dharma. Bhima
and Arjuna, as Indra and Vayu, embody strength and
valor, with Bhima's physical power and Arjuna's skill
in archery symbolizing divine forces at work. In
contrast, the Kauravas are likened to reptilian asuras,
bound by ego and greed, and collectively
representing the forces of darkness and ignorance.

Draupadi as the earth is significant, portraying her as
the essence of fertility and sacrifice, enduring the
suffering caused by humanity's choices. Her plight
represents the exploitation and suffering of nature
under the forces of material greed and disharmony.
Her rescue and protection become the ultimate goal
of the Pandavas, indicating the duty of humanity to
safeguard the earth and uphold balance against the
forces of disharmony.

सूर्यपुत्रो मित्र: देवानां द्रौपदी दुर्गा एको शक्तिः |
साक्षी यमो विदुरः तस्य पुत्रो :युधिष्ठिरः मनुः ||23||

Karna is the Mitra among the gods; Draupadi, as
Durga, is the single unifying power. Yama is Vidura,
the witness, whose son, Yudhishthira, embodies
humanity.
Karna, as Mitra, symbolizes the solar, compassionate
aspect that maintains cosmic order, despite being
isolated by circumstances. His life reflects loyalty and

adherence to duty, even at the cost of personal sacrifice. Draupadi as Durga suggests a convergence of divine power within her, signifying the singular force of resilience and protection in times of crisis, uniting all forces to defend Dharma.

Vidura, as Yama's manifestation, serves as a neutral observer of Dharma, embodying wisdom and justice. His association with Yudhishthira represents humanity's moral compass. Yudhishthira, as Vidura's son, inherits a sense of justice and humanity's potential for Dharma, becoming the spiritual touchstone amidst the trials of the Mahabharata, showing how individuals must align with higher moral principles.

वृष्णि कुलेषु जातो नारायणस्य चतुर्व्युहः |
वासुदेवः बलरामो प्रद्युम्नो अनिरुद्धः ||24||

In the Vrishni clan, Narayana was born with his fourfold deities: Vasudeva, Balarama, Pradyumna, and Aniruddha.
This verse speaks to Krishna's divine nature, reflecting the fourfold expansion of Narayana as a cosmic protector. Vasudeva, Krishna's earthly form, represents the guiding wisdom that leads humanity; Balarama, his elder brother, embodies physical strength and righteousness; Pradyumna represents creative intelligence, and Aniruddha signifies self-

control and perseverance.

Together, these aspects reveal the qualities necessary to lead humanity toward harmony and spiritual evolution. Krishna's incarnation in the Vrishni clan symbolizes how divinity manifests among humans to restore balance, embodying qualities needed to guide society toward inner and outer peace.

अनिरुद्धस्य पुत्रो वज्रो उषापतिः भविष्यति |
नूतनवंशस्य आरब्धः कलौ अन्ते करिष्यति ||25||

Aniruddha's son, Vajra, will marry Usha, beginning a new lineage at the end of Kali Yuga.
This prophecy refers to the cycle of regeneration after the age of conflict (Kali Yuga), when humanity's potential for divinity will be renewed. Vajra represents a purified energy born from divine intervention, embodying a future humanity untainted by ego. His marriage to Usha, symbolizing dawn or a new beginning, indicates a rebirth of values and purity in a future age.

Their union initiates a lineage that will lead humanity beyond Kali Yuga's darkness, suggesting a gradual restoration of divine qualities. This union signals hope and spiritual renewal, symbolizing humanity's return to a higher path after cycles of ignorance.

वंशैतत् दिव्यमानसः जायमानः युद्धान्तरे |
अमराः अभौतिकाः च मायायाः परे स्थिताः ||26||

This race of divine humanity will form after the end of this great war symbolized in the Mahabharata. That humanity will be immortal, non-physical, and beyond illusory Maya.
The verse points to a transformed human race emerging after the conflict, a humanity that is beyond the confines of material limitations and immersed in divine consciousness. This future race is characterized by spiritual immortality and a transcendence of worldly illusions, marking an era of purity and higher awareness.

This new humanity, freed from the limitations of Maya, signifies the blossoming of consciousness where individuals transcend ego, seeing the universe as interconnected and living. The Mahabharata's great war represents an inner battle within the soul to overcome materiality and evolve toward spiritual enlightenment.

युद्धान्तरः युगान्तरः असुरलोकस्य अन्तः |
युधिष्ठिरस्य स्वर्गमनं मानवानां अमृतं इति ||27||

The end of war is the end of an eon, which marks the end of the asura-dominated earth. This is the entry of Yudhishthira into heaven and signifies the immortality of humans.

The verse suggests that the conclusion of the Mahabharata war symbolizes not only a physical battle but the closing of a dark epoch. Yudhishthira's ascension to heaven represents humanity's potential for attaining higher states of consciousness and a purified existence, free from the cycle of death and rebirth.

The "end of the asura-dominated earth" implies a shift from materialistic to spiritual values. Humanity's collective consciousness moves towards a state of liberation, embodying immortality in the form of spiritual awakening and freedom from the cycles of ego-driven conflicts.

भारतनाम्ना नाटकस्य कविः व्यासो हरिः |
नर्तयन्ति सर्वाः देवाः असुराः तत् अक्षसंख्येषु ||28||

The poet of this Bharata play is Vyasa, who is Vishnu himself. All gods and demons dance on the dice rolls of this play.

This verse emphasizes the "Mahabharata" as a divine drama, orchestrated by Vyasa, an avatar of Vishnu. The gods and demons are like characters on a grand stage, each playing their roles according to the cosmic dice of fate. This indicates that the events of the Mahabharata are not random but divinely choreographed.

The "dance on the dice rolls" symbolizes how each being's fate is interwoven into a cosmic game beyond individual control. Vyasa, as the poet and orchestrator, is aware of every consequence, showing how the divine will underpins even chaotic moments, steering all toward a higher

द्युतक्रिडा आद्यपिठ: चित्शक्त्यः कालचक्रस्य |
वृणोति तां भाग्यवन्तां कारकानां कर्माणां ||29||

The game of dice is the original stage of consciousness and the power behind the wheel of time. The Lord chooses those fortunate ones who understand the true doer behind all karmas.
This verse suggests that the dice game in the Mahabharata symbolizes the unfolding of cosmic consciousness within the cycle of time. The wheel of time turns based on the karmas of all beings, where each soul plays its part according to its deeds. Those who understand the divine orchestration behind actions are considered fortunate, as they grasp the essence of karma—the unseen force guiding existence.

To recognize the divine as the ultimate doer is to transcend the illusions of ego and personal will. When one understands that the cosmic play is directed by a higher consciousness, they find peace in surrendering to the divine will. This understanding grants them freedom from attachment to outcomes, aligning their actions with cosmic harmony.

संख्येषु असंख्येषु या या गति भवेत् जीवस्य |
मत्वा तत् सौभाग्यं सा सा कर्मगतिम् चरेत् ||30||

The fate of each soul is determined by countless dice rolls. Knowing this secret, one should align their actions accordingly.
This verse emphasizes the idea of karma as a vast and intricate web, where every action contributes to a soul's destiny. Each soul's journey, shaped by infinite karmic consequences, is like a series of dice rolls in the game of life. By recognizing this truth, one gains insight into their karmic path and learns to act with awareness, embracing their role in the cosmic order.

This understanding encourages individuals to perform their duties selflessly, knowing that the divine is the ultimate orchestrator. By aligning one's actions with the understanding of karmic law, they are liberated from the bondage of karma and can navigate life with clarity and balance.

मनसः त्रिभागाः सन्ति काव्यतर्कमीमांसा |

चतुर्थं मनः देवमनः सरस्वत्याः प्रचोदितः ||31||

There are three levels of the lower mind—inspiration, logic, and analysis. The fourth level is the divine mind, which is the realm of Saraswati.
This verse reveals a hierarchy of mental faculties, moving from inspiration and logic to a deeper analytical capacity. The lower mind operates within these domains, addressing the intellectual and imaginative aspects of life. However, the highest state is the divine mind, an intuitive, transcendent consciousness guided by Saraswati, the goddess of wisdom and knowledge.

The divine mind represents insight beyond logic and rational thought. It is the seat of intuitive wisdom, transcending the limitations of the lower mind. By cultivating Saraswati's divine guidance, one attains clarity, perceiving truth beyond ordinary perception, thus accessing the infinite depths of cosmic wisdom.

कालो अधुना देवमनसः ईळस्य सुपर्णस्य |
तत् वर्तते द्युतेषु विना तर्केण विना सता ||32||

Now is the time of the divine mind, under the guidance of Lord Ila. This mind functions as a dice game, without logic and proof.
The verse suggests a cosmic shift, where the divine

mind (deva manas) is becoming predominant, guided by Lord Ila, a form of Vishnu representing universal harmony. This mind operates beyond human reasoning, functioning more like the throw of a dice in the game of life, unfathomable and without conventional logic.

This time marks a transition to a mode of understanding that relies on intuition and surrender to divine will rather than analytical thinking. It invites us to trust in the unseen, accepting that the mysteries of existence unfold beyond human comprehension, in the hands of divine intelligence.

अक्षक्रीडाम् अनुवर्तमानाः सुयोधनधर्मयोः |
नागाः गरुडाः खेलयन्ति जयार्थं पृथिव्याः ||33||

The dice game between Duryodhana and Yudhisthira symbolizes a cosmic struggle. In reality, reptilian Nagas and celestial Garudas play for the earth's dominion.
This verse portrays the Mahabharata's central conflict as a symbolic battle between Nagas (representing static, binding forces) and Garudas (embodying dynamic, liberating forces). Duryodhana and Yudhisthira become avatars for these ancient cosmic energies vying for influence over the earth.

The dice game is thus not merely a dispute between humans but a reflection of the perpetual struggle between darkness and light, ignorance and wisdom, stagnation and evolution. The battlefield becomes a theater for these energies to play out their roles in the cycle of creation, each seeking victory over earthly realms.

नागाः दितिपुत्राः सन्ति गरुडाः आदित्या दिवो |
वैरं तेषाम प्राचीनं युगान्ते वर्तयिष्यति ||34||

Naga reptilians are children of Diti, while Garuda eagles are children of Aditi. Their ancient enmity continues throughout the ages.
This verse describes the ancient cosmic rivalry between the forces born of Diti and Aditi, representing asuras and devas, respectively. The Nagas (reptilian forces) and Garudas (celestial eagle forces) embody opposing energies that perpetually clash across yugas (ages), symbolizing the endless duality within creation.

This enmity between the static and the dynamic, the material and the spiritual, is central to cosmic balance. Each yuga revisits this struggle, revealing it as a constant process in the evolution of the universe where opposing forces maintain the fabric of existence.

नागानां वासुकी राजा देवानां वृत्रघ्नः तथा |
हन्त्वर्थं वृत्रसर्पस्य विष्णो भवति तस्य सखा ||35||

Vasuki is the king of the Nagas, and Indra is the king of the devas. To defeat the Naga influence, Vishnu becomes an ally of Indra.

This verse illustrates Vishnu's role as a divine mediator, aiding Indra in the battle against the negative influences symbolized by the Nagas. Vasuki, representing the Nagas, embodies the binding, restrictive forces, while Indra and Vishnu symbolize liberation and transformation.

Vishnu's alliance with Indra suggests that divine intervention supports the forces of evolution when material forces attempt to dominate. Through Vishnu's guidance, these liberating forces strive to restore balance, maintaining the cosmic order against static, regressive influences.

नागाः स्थितिरुपाः बलः पक्षिणाः गतिबलः |
एको यतन्ति रुपान्तरार्थं असुरः साम्यार्थं ||36||

Nagas represent static power, while Garudas represent dynamic, moving power. One seeks to evolve, while the other seeks to maintain the status quo.

This verse highlights the duality between Nagas and Garudas, representing the contrast between stasis and movement. Nagas symbolize the forces that aim to preserve the existing order, while Garudas embody the forces that seek transformation and evolution.

This interplay of static and dynamic is a fundamental part of the universe, where evolution is driven by the tension between forces that resist change and those that promote it. Together, they sustain the balance of creation, each playing an essential role in the cosmic design.

युद्धे ताभ्यां युगे ग्रहे कालचक्रः प्रवर्तयति |
नागाः हन्ति पक्षिणाम् ते खादयति नागान् ||37||

In the war between them in this Yuga and on this planet, the wheel of time turns. Nagas kill Garudas, and Garudas consume Nagas.
The verse speaks of the eternal cycle of conflict between static and dynamic forces, symbolized by the Nagas and Garudas. This cyclical struggle, occurring throughout the ages and realms, reflects the ongoing balance maintained by destruction and regeneration.

As each force counteracts the other, the wheel of time (kala chakra) continues its course. This constant interplay of opposition and assimilation drives evolution, where one force momentarily triumphs, only to be counterbalanced by its opposite, keeping the universe in perpetual motion.

नाटके अस्मिन् भारते को जितः को अजितः |
को जानाति विना कृष्णेन कृष्णोऽपि अज्ञः इव ||38||

In this play of the Mahabharata, who wins and who loses? Who knows, except Krishna? Or perhaps Krishna himself is unaware.
This verse raises a philosophical question about victory and defeat, suggesting that in the grand cosmic drama, ultimate outcomes may be beyond human understanding. Even Krishna, the orchestrator, is depicted as detached, indifferent to human notions of winning or losing.

This ambiguity points to the futility of judging success by worldly standards. It underscores that the cosmic play transcends human dualities, where victory and defeat are relative. Ultimately, it is Krishna alone who knows or may not know

सारथि सः विना शस्त्रेण आलोकयति युद्धं |
चेतकः तेषां बुद्धियः न हन्ति हन्ता सर्वाणां ||39||

Krishna is the driver of the vehicle, observing the war without wielding any weapon. He inspires their actions —though he does not kill, he orchestrates the fate of all.

This verse reflects Krishna's role as the charioteer for Arjuna, where he remains weaponless yet influences the entire course of the Mahabharata war. His mere presence provides direction and courage to Arjuna and inspires the Pandavas in their righteous battle. Krishna, though not physically engaged in combat, is the catalyst for transformation, subtly guiding actions and decisions.

Krishna's influence signifies divine intervention that operates beyond direct action. He embodies the concept of an inner guide, the charioteer of the soul, who directs without coercion. By empowering others to act according to their Dharma, he serves as both the witness and the unseen force behind every outcome in the cosmic play of life.

सैन्यं अदत्तं दुर्योधनं सा भौतिका शक्तिः महान् |
देवमनः कृष्णः सुपर्णः सारथि अभूत धर्मस्य ||40||

He bestowed upon Duryodhana great physical power —his army, representing today's science and technology. The divine mind, Krishna, the eagle, became the charioteer of Yudhishthira's brother. This verse suggests that Duryodhana's army, symbolizing material strength and technological prowess, was his main source of power. Duryodhana represents the embodiment of physical strength and ambition, fueled by external, worldly forces. In contrast, Krishna as the divine mind (devamana) serves as Arjuna's guide, symbolizing spiritual wisdom and moral guidance over sheer physical prowess.

The juxtaposition of material strength with divine guidance underscores the Mahabharata's theme of Dharma versus adharma. While Duryodhana's reliance on physical power leads to his downfall, Krishna's guidance aligns the Pandavas with cosmic truth, highlighting the limitations of material power when not anchored in spiritual wisdom.

शतनागाः रुद्रप्रजा भुतशास्त्रे पारङ्गताः |
वसन्ति पाताललोकेषु भूगर्भे पर्वतगुहासु ||41||

The hundred Nagas, sons of Rudra, are experts in physical sciences. They dwell in the underworld, in deep caves within the earth's mountains.
This verse introduces the Nagas, progeny of Rudra, who are skilled in the physical sciences and reside within the earth's subterranean realms. As masters of the physical plane, they represent the hidden, esoteric knowledge of material reality. Their association with Rudra connects them to the primal forces of nature and the mysteries hidden within the earth.

Dwelling in deep, secluded places, the Nagas signify the concealed wisdom of the material world, accessible only through inner exploration or spiritual guidance. They symbolize the potent, often misunderstood forces of nature that lie beneath the surface of conscious awareness, embodying the unmanifest potential of creation.

पञ्चदेवाः दक्षप्रजा मानसशास्त्राणां सिद्धाः |
सूक्ष्मलोके वसन्ति ते ध्रुवे उत्तरेषु सदा ||42||

Five types of beings, the progeny of Daksha, are well-versed in the sciences of the mind. They reside in subtle realms around the north pole.
This verse speaks of the five divine races created by Daksha, who are adept in mental sciences and live in subtle, elevated realms near the north pole, symbolizing regions of spiritual knowledge. These beings have evolved beyond physical limitations, representing advanced forms of consciousness dedicated to intellectual and mental pursuits.

Their location in subtle realms suggests that they are beyond the reach of ordinary human perception. They embody refined aspects of knowledge, especially related to the mind, serving as guides or archetypes for those who seek to transcend material limitations and attain higher understanding.

गुहावासिनः रुद्राः यज्ञस्य सदा शत्रवः |
यज्ञं रूपान्तरं लोकस्य वाचो प्राणो हविः ||43||

The Rudras who dwell in caves are perpetual enemies of sacrifice. Sacrifice is the transformation of the world, where speech and prana are the offerings. The Rudras, residing in seclusion, represent forces that challenge or disrupt the process of sacrifice. Sacrifice (yajna) here symbolizes transformation and evolution, where elements of speech (vak) and vital energy (prana) serve as sacred offerings in the cosmic process. The Rudras' resistance reflects the natural tension between transformation and stasis within the universe.

The verse points to a deeper truth: the Rudras' opposition to yajna serves to test and strengthen the resolve of those performing the sacrifice. Their role is necessary in the grand cosmic play, as they ensure that the transformative process remains pure, not corrupted by weakness or complacency.

दक्षो कृतवान् यज्ञं पुरा चक्रस्य भ्रमणार्थे |
रुद्रो विविनाश तं इन्द्रविष्णुभ्यः जितवान ||44||

Daksha once performed a sacrifice to set the cycle of evolution in motion. Rudra destroyed that sacrifice, triumphing over Indra and Vishnu.
This verse recalls the story of Daksha's yajna, a ritual intended to drive the cosmic cycle forward. However, Rudra, representing primal forces resistant to

transformation, disrupts this sacrifice. His triumph over Indra and Vishnu suggests that even the highest cosmic powers cannot override the will of Rudra, embodying the untamable, chaotic aspect of the divine.

Rudra's destruction of the sacrifice signifies that transformation requires balance with primal forces. His intervention shows that evolution cannot proceed without respect for the wild, uncontrollable energies that must be integrated and honored within the process.

रुद्रः भुतसृष्टिकर्ता स्थावरपशुपर्यन्तं |
सः खलु पशुपति लोके सप्त भुवनेषु सदा ||45||

Rudra is the creator of all beings, from the earth to animals. He is indeed the lord of all creatures across the seven worlds.
This verse highlights Rudra's role as the primal creator, responsible for the emergence of life from the earth to the animal kingdom. Known as Pashupati (Lord of Animals), he governs not only physical beings but also the elemental forces across the seven planes of existence, embodying the untamed, natural energy that sustains life.

Rudra's domain over all creatures signifies his integral role in the cycle of birth, death, and rebirth. His influence pervades every aspect of existence, ensuring the continuity of life and the preservation of the natural world. He is both the creator and protector of primal, elemental forces within the cosmos.

हिमालये च कैलासे पाताले हाटकनामे |
राजति गुहासु तेषु यज्ञध्वन्सि उमापतिः ||46||

In the Himalayas, at Kailasa, and in the underworld called Hataka, the destroyer of sacrifices, the lord of Uma, resides in those caves.
This verse describes Rudra's dwelling places, from the heights of Kailasa to the subterranean realms of Hataka, indicating his vast and encompassing presence across realms. Known as the destroyer of sacrifices, he resides with Uma, embodying the union of destructive and nurturing forces, balancing the forces of creation and dissolution.

His presence in remote, hidden regions signifies his connection to the mysteries of existence, untouched by the ordinary rituals of society. Rudra's abode symbolizes a return to primal consciousness, where the dual forces of creation and destruction coexist in harmony, governed by the wisdom of the eternal.

यक्षरक्षां प्राणसृष्टिः देवासुराः मनुप्रजा |
चतुस्रष्टा पिता ब्रह्मा द्युलोके नभे स्थितः ||47||

Brahma, the creator of the four species—Yakshas and Rakshasas (vital beings), Devas and Asuras, and humanity—resides in the celestial realms.
This verse acknowledges Brahma as the creator of the primary races within Hindu cosmology: the Yakshas and Rakshasas (associated with vital energy), the Devas and Asuras (representing light and darkness), and humans. These races embody various aspects of existence, each serving a role within the cosmic order, illustrating the diversity of creation.

Brahma's residence in the celestial realms reflects his role as the overseer of existence, impartially creating the forces that animate the universe. His presence in the heavens symbolizes the divine intelligence that initiates and sustains life, giving each being its unique role in the cosmic drama.

चतुर्मुखेषु चतुः जाता चतुर्वेदा चतुर्वंशाः |
पञ्चम कर्षयति रुद्रो पुरा गुप्तहेतवे ||48||

From Brahma's four heads emerged the four Vedas and the four primary races. Rudra removed the fifth

for a hidden purpose.
This verse highlights Brahma as the creator of both sacred knowledge (the Vedas) and the human races. Each of the Vedas corresponds to different aspects of wisdom, and the four races represent distinct archetypes within society. However, Rudra's removal of the fifth aspect suggests a hidden path or wisdom that remains concealed, accessible only to those who delve deeply into the mysteries of existence.

Rudra's act points to the existence of esoteric knowledge, reserved for the initiated. This hidden knowledge hints at an advanced spiritual understanding that transcends ordinary wisdom and integrates the deeper aspects of creation. It emphasizes that enlightenment requires confronting and embracing Rudra's transformative energy.

पशुपति भूतस्रष्टा मनप्राणजगतां कः |
तमरजतुलाकर्ता सत्वो नारायणो महः ||49||

The Lord of animals is the creator of elemental beings, while Brahma forms the world of mind and prana. Narayana, embodying Satwa, balances the creation of Tamas and Rajas.
This verse describes the roles of divine figures in the cosmos. Rudra (Pashupati) oversees the creation of primal life forms, Brahma shapes realms of mental and vital energies, and Narayana (Vishnu) maintains

harmony by balancing the qualities of Tamas (inertia) and Rajas (activity) with Satwa (purity).

Narayana's role as the harmonizer of Tamas and Rajas highlights his function as a stabilizing force, guiding creation toward evolution and balance. His presence ensures that creation moves steadily toward enlightenment, integrating various aspects of existence into a cohesive whole.

चतुर्वंशाः त्रिगुणाः द्वादशाकृतिः दिवसृष्टि ।
पञ्चपादाः त्रिगुणाः पञ्चदशी भूतसृष्टि ॥50॥

The four races, three qualities, and twelve forms make up the immortal world. Fivefold beings with triple qualities create the fifteen-fold realm of animals. This verse delves into the structure of creation. The immortal world, comprised of divine or enlightened beings, is formed through the combination of four races and three qualities, resulting in twelve archetypes. The mortal world, particularly the animal realm, operates within a framework of five primary forms and three qualities, resulting in fifteen archetypes.

The verse reveals the layered complexity of existence, where various combinations of qualities and archetypes form distinct realms of life. This cosmic structure reflects how different expressions of life emerge from divine energies, shaping both the physical and spiritual worlds.

देवासुरसंग्रामे तथा पक्षिनागाभ्यां |
कुरुपाण्डवयो मध्ये एका सा भारती कथा ||51||

The battle between Devas and Asuras parallels the war between Nagas (reptilians) and Garudas (angels), and also between the Kauravas and Pandavas. This is the story of Bharata.
This verse draws parallels between various cosmic conflicts, indicating that the battle between light and darkness is a recurring theme. The Devas and Asuras represent forces of light and shadow, the Nagas and Garudas represent opposing primal energies, and the Kauravas and Pandavas embody this cosmic struggle on the human plane.

The Mahabharata, or "Bharata" story, thus becomes a microcosm of the universal struggle between conflicting forces. It reveals the inherent duality within creation, where opposing energies drive the evolution of consciousness. Each of these battles represents a phase in the soul's journey toward unity and balance.

कथा एतत् मनुष्याणां पूर्वानां नवागतानां |
चतुर्वणाः तेषु देहेषु त्रिगुणेभिः वर्तत्यन्ति ||52||

The story of Bharata is about humans who were born in the past and those who will be born in the future. The four varnas operate within each body through a combination of the three qualities.
This verse emphasizes that the Mahabharata's lessons transcend time, speaking to humanity's past, present, and future. Each individual embodies a combination of the three qualities—Satwa, Rajas, and Tamas—within their varna (societal role or archetype), which shapes their character and destiny.

The interplay of varna and guna (qualities) represents the diverse expressions of Dharma (duty) within humanity. It reminds us that each person's path and purpose are unique, shaped by a blend of inherited qualities and their place within the broader cosmic structure. The story of Bharata thus serves as an eternal guide for understanding individual nature and fulfilling one's role in the cosmic order.

यत् यत् वर्णः यद् गुणं वर्तति तत् जीवेषु |
तत् तस्य धर्मः लोके स्वभावः इति कथ्यते ||53||

The combination of varna (color or class) and guna (quality) forms the nature of each soul's body. This combination determines their dharma, which is called the person's inherent nature in society.
This verse explains how each person's dharma, or

duty, is shaped by their varna and guna. These qualities determine not only a person's role in society but also their inner nature or swabhava. Dharma, therefore, is not an imposed rule but an expression of one's true self, rooted in the combination of one's qualities and societal role.

Following one's natural dharma brings harmony within oneself and with the world. The verse emphasizes the importance of self-awareness and alignment with one's true nature, as this is the path to fulfilling one's purpose and contributing positively to society and the cosmos.

स्वभावेषु निधनं श्रेयः परभावः भयावहः |
स्वधर्मो आचरयित्वा प्राप्स्यते स्वर्गो महत् ||54||

It is better to die following one's own nature; adopting another's nature brings fear and harm. By following one's own dharma according to varna and guna, one attains true heaven.
This verse advises adherence to one's own dharma (swadharma), as embracing another's nature can lead to confusion and inner conflict. The path of swadharma is rooted in one's unique qualities and role, providing a sense of purpose and direction. Acting outside this alignment leads to disharmony and, ultimately, fear and suffering.

The verse implies that true liberation (heaven) comes from fulfilling one's innate purpose rather than imitating others. By staying true to one's dharma, an individual contributes to the harmony of the whole and experiences a sense of fulfillment and peace.

प्रकृतिज: स्वभावः सा प्रकृति त्रिगुणात्मिका |
सत्वरजतमसाकृतिभिः सा भवति चतुर्देहेषु ||55||

Nature is born of Prakriti, which is composed of the three gunas (qualities). Through Satwa, Rajas, and Tamas, she forms the four varna bodies.
This verse delves into the origins of individual nature, explaining that Prakriti (the primal nature) is the source of all individual characteristics. The interplay of Satwa (purity), Rajas (activity), and Tamas (inertia) manifests as the four varnas (societal archetypes or classes), shaping human diversity.

Prakriti, as the cosmic mother, forms each individual's unique constitution, directing them toward a particular path within society. This cosmic structure emphasizes that each person's characteristics and purpose arise from the primordial balance of the three qualities, affirming the harmony within diversity in creation.

असङ्ख्याः जीवाः भवति द्वादशयोगेभिः |
तेषां स्वभावजं कर्म तेषां धर्म उच्यते ||56||

Innumerable souls are created by the multiplication of four varnas with three gunas, forming twelve archetypes. The karma arising from their nature is called their dharma.
This verse illustrates the complexity of creation, where the combination of varnas and gunas results in twelve distinct archetypes. Each soul, shaped by its unique blend of qualities, follows a specific karmic path, which becomes its dharma. This karma, rooted in each being's inherent nature, defines its responsibilities and purpose within the cosmic order.

The verse implies that dharma is not a rigid set of rules but a natural expression of one's inner qualities. By understanding and embracing their dharma, individuals align themselves with their true nature, contributing to the harmony and evolution of the universe

कर्तारः ते कर्माणां फ़लम् हि ईश्वराय अर्पिताः |
ज्ञात्वा अहं यन्त्रः खलु कर्ता यन्त्रि वासुदेवः ||57||

They should perform karma by offering its results to the supreme Lord, realizing that they are merely instruments, with Vasudeva as the true operator.
This verse encourages a profound attitude of surrender, where individuals understand themselves

as instruments or "robots" in the hands of the divine. The true essence of karma lies in dedicating all actions and their outcomes to the Supreme, recognizing that it is not the individual self but Vasudeva who ultimately controls every movement.

This perspective fosters detachment, as one's ego dissolves into the recognition of divine orchestration. When one surrenders to Vasudeva's will, their actions transcend personal desires, achieving a higher alignment with cosmic purpose. This surrender brings liberation from the bondage of karma, as the individual acts without attachment.

न बध्नाति तां कर्माणि ये कृता देवभावे |
सः खलु कर्मसन्यासः न च मुण्डी न च दण्डी ||58||

Karmas performed with a sense of divine possession do not bind the doer. This is true renunciation; simply becoming an ascetic is not genuine sannyasa.
This verse redefines sannyasa (renunciation) as a state of being rather than a mere lifestyle choice. When one performs actions while feeling infused with divine consciousness, they become liberated from the karmic bonds that typically accompany such actions. True sannyasa, therefore, is not in external symbols like a shaved head or staff, but in a state of mind that remains unattached to the results of actions.

This insight underscores that real renunciation is

internal—it is the attitude of acting as a channel for divine will. By living in a state of divine possession, individuals transcend ego, becoming vessels of the divine purpose, free from the binding effects of karma

एषः कथितः कर्मयोगः कर्मक्षेत्रे धर्मक्षेत्रे |
येन पार्थो असंशयात्मा हन्ति कौरवान् शतान् ||59||

This karma yoga was taught on the field of karma, the earth, which is also the field of Dharma. Through this yoga, Arjuna dispelled his doubts and defeated the hundred Kauravas.
The verse recalls how the teachings of karma yoga, imparted on the battlefield of Kurukshetra, enabled Arjuna to overcome his doubts and fulfill his role as a warrior. Earth is both a karma-kshetra (field of action) and a dharma-kshetra (field of righteousness), where individuals face the dual challenge of acting while upholding moral principles.
Karma yoga provided Arjuna with the clarity to transcend his attachments and execute his dharma without fear or hesitation. This teaching is universal, guiding each individual to act with purpose and without attachment to outcomes, achieving peace and alignment with the cosmic order
योगः कर्मसु कुशलं कर्म; तत् स्वभावजं |
ज्ञात्वा स्वस्वभावं तत् नैषकर्म्यं योगः कथ्यते ||60

Yoga is expertise in karma, which arises from one's

true nature (swabhava). Knowing one's swabhava and acting accordingly is called Naishkarmya yoga. This verse emphasizes that yoga is skillfulness in action, which comes from understanding and aligning with one's innate nature (swabhava). When actions arise from true self-awareness, one achieves Naishkarmya yoga—a state of action without karmic bondage. This yoga is not about avoiding work but about performing it in alignment with one's essence.

Naishkarmya yoga teaches that liberation is achieved through actions performed in harmony with one's true nature. By knowing oneself and acting accordingly, individuals experience fulfillment and freedom, transcending the cycle of karma.

कृत्वा अपि विना कर्तृभावं तत्भाव देवेषु स्थितः |
देवभावं आवेशे शरीरे योग: भवति महान् ||61||

Expanded Interpretation:
By acting without the notion of personal doership and by embodying the divine presence within, karma yoga occurs when one is possessed by a deity or higher force.
This verse reveals that true karma yoga occurs when the individual ego is absent, and one acts as an instrument of divine power. When a person is "possessed" or deeply aligned with a deity or higher consciousness, they operate beyond personal motives, guided by divine will.

This state of divine possession elevates ordinary actions to a level of sacredness, as the individual becomes a channel for divine purpose. The essence of yoga here lies in surrendering personal identity, allowing the divine to work through the physical form in perfect harmony.

सः योगः यज्ञः प्रोक्तः येन भ्रमति कालचक्रं |
रूपान्तरं प्राणिनाम् मानवानां सद्गतिः ||62||

This yoga is called the sacrifice through which the wheel of time moves, enabling the transformation of all species toward a divine state of true mind-born beings.
This verse likens karma yoga to a cosmic sacrifice (yajna) that fuels the movement of time (kala chakra) and drives the evolution of consciousness. Through this sacred act of selfless action, all beings gradually transform, evolving toward a divine state where they embody the mind-born essence of the true self.

This ongoing sacrifice sustains and propels the universe, reflecting the eternal cycle of creation, preservation, and transformation. By engaging in this yoga, humans participate in the cosmic process, advancing their own spiritual journey and contributing to the evolution of all life forms.

स्वभावाः द्वादशाः नवरसभेदेन नटयन्ति |
बृहति ते अक्षसुत्रैः वेदरसमुर्तिसङ्ख्यया ||63||

Twelve swabhavas (innate natures) play out with
combinations of nine rasas (emotions) on the dice of
numbers symbolized in the Veda's essence and
structure.
This verse explores the concept of human nature
(swabhava) as a blend of twelve archetypes, each
interacting with the nine fundamental emotions
(rasas). These archetypes play out on the "dice" of
cosmic numbers, reflecting the structured diversity
inherent in the Vedas, which represent the blueprint of
universal knowledge and experience.

The verse suggests that each person's life unfolds as
a dynamic interplay of these archetypes and
emotions, guided by the divine wisdom encoded in
the Vedic structure. This view sees human existence
as a dance between innate qualities and experiences,
illustrating the complexity and richness of the soul's
journey.

नर्तकामात्राः मानवाः पीठेषु देशेषु पृथिव्यौ |
देवासुराः खेलयन्ति द्रौपद्यार्थं द्युतक्रीडा ||64||

Humans are actors on the stage of Jambu Island

(earth). Devas and Asuras play by possessing human bodies to win Draupadi, symbolizing the victory over earth.

This verse presents humanity as actors on the grand stage of life, with Devas (gods) and Asuras (demons) acting through them. The struggle between these divine and demonic forces, embodied by the humans they influence, symbolizes the eternal battle for the earth's soul, represented by Draupadi.

This metaphor highlights the spiritual battle within each individual, where divine and demonic tendencies vie for control. Draupadi, as a symbol of the earth, represents the prize of self-mastery and alignment with Dharma. The verse underscores that life is a cosmic play, with each soul embodying and expressing these opposing forces.

द्रौपदी हि अग्निकन्या धेनुः शक्तिः वाक् दुर्गा |
यया वृणितः ते धन्याः पृथिव्याः सम्राटः ||65||

Draupadi is the daughter of fire, representing the cow, the power of speech, and Durga. Whoever wins her becomes the emperor of the earth.

This verse describes Draupadi as a divine feminine archetype, embodying the elements of fire, purity, speech (vak), and Durga's protective power. She represents the sacred, life-sustaining essence of the earth, embodying wisdom, strength, and resilience. The one who "wins" Draupadi, meaning who understands and respects her power, gains mastery over the earth itself.

Draupadi symbolizes the unity of spirit and matter, a bridge between divine wisdom and earthly existence. To attain her favor is to align with cosmic principles, achieving sovereignty over one's self and the world through harmony with divine truth

सा अवृणोत पाण्डवान् स्वयंवरेषु तस्याः पुरा |
तदपि नागाः भोगार्थे गृह्णीयात् तां बलात् ||66||

In ancient times, Draupadi chose the Pandavas as her lords, yet the Nagas (reptilians) took her by force for their enjoyment.
This verse reflects the story of Draupadi's choice and subsequent abduction, symbolizing the ongoing struggle between divine and material forces. Draupadi's choice of the Pandavas as her protectors signifies her alignment with righteousness and dharma. However, the Nagas represent forces of selfish desire, symbolizing the darker, material aspects that seek to control and exploit divine wisdom and feminine power for personal gain.

This conflict highlights the tension between spiritual aspirations and worldly temptations. Draupadi embodies the purity and sanctity of Earth and the divine feminine, which must be defended from exploitation by forces that seek to misuse her power. This battle over Draupadi reflects the broader cosmic struggle for control of the Earth and its spiritual treasures.

सा पुरा प्रतिज्ञाता स्म सप्तशत्यौ य कथिता |
सप्तशति कथा युद्धस्य शक्त्यः रहस्यस्य ||67||

Expanded Interpretation:
Long ago, she took a vow described in a seven-hundred-verse text, known as the story of the war of Shaktis, containing many secrets of divine powers. This verse alludes to the "Saptashati," a sacred text dedicated to the goddess Durga, which contains seven hundred verses detailing the power, battles, and mysteries of Shaktis (divine feminine powers). Draupadi, as an incarnation of Durga, took a vow of self-defense and empowerment, expressing her commitment to resisting forces of ignorance and protecting Dharma.

The "Saptashati" embodies hidden wisdom and the transformative power of the divine feminine. It teaches that true strength lies in purity and alignment with Dharma, and it holds the keys to overcoming obstacles through inner empowerment and devotion. Draupadi's vow signifies her dedication to these principles and her role as a protector of cosmic balance.

यो मे जयति संग्रामे यो मे दर्पं व्यपोहति |
यो मे प्रतिबलो लोके स मे भर्ता भविष्यति ||68||

The one who wins me in battle, who humbles my pride, and who matches my power shall be my lord, declares Draupadi-Durga.
This verse captures Draupadi's challenge to the world, stating that only a true equal—one who can defeat her in battle, humble her pride, and stand as her counterpart in power and spirit—shall become her lord. This test is not merely physical but spiritual, requiring alignment with her virtues of courage, purity, and wisdom.

Draupadi represents the cosmic feminine power, and her statement reflects the high standards of Dharma. It signifies that to attain unity with divine power, one must cultivate qualities of strength, humility, and balance. Her challenge serves as a reminder that spiritual union is a matter of inner alignment, where true power lies in overcoming ego and embodying virtue.

देवासुराणां कुरुपण्डुनां यो जयति कृष्णां दुर्गां |
शासन्ति ते त्रिलोके सदा एतत् शास्त्रस्य निर्णयः ||69||

Between the Devas and Asuras, the Kauravas and Pandavas, whoever conquers the dark Durga (Draupadi) will rule the three worlds—this is the essence of the teaching.
This verse reveals the cosmic stakes of the Mahabharata conflict. Draupadi, as an incarnation of Durga, represents the Earth's sovereignty and the potential for enlightenment. The victor in this divine struggle, whether among Devas and Asuras or Kauravas and Pandavas, attains rulership over the three worlds (heaven, earth, and the underworld).

This teaching emphasizes that true dominion over the cosmos requires mastery over the ego and alignment with cosmic Dharma. Draupadi as "dark Durga" represents the power of transformation and the capacity to balance light and shadow. Victory in this spiritual battle signifies achieving harmony within the self and alignment with the divine order.

अक्षोभिः खेलायिन्ताः ते युध्यर्थं आगता तदा |
भीमार्जुनैः जितवान् ; सः अगमत् स्वर्गेषु तदा ||70||

They came to win this war by playing with dice, but Bhima and Arjuna defeated them, and Yudhishthira ascended to the heavens.
This verse reflects the events of the Mahabharata, where the Kauravas and Pandavas engage in a cosmic battle that begins with a game of dice. Despite the Kauravas' efforts to manipulate and dominate, Bhima and Arjuna ultimately triumph in battle, leading Yudhishthira to ascend to the heavens as a symbol of spiritual liberation.

The transition from the dice game to the battlefield symbolizes life's progression from fate-driven challenges to conscious, decisive action. Yudhishthira's ascent represents the soul's journey toward enlightenment, transcending worldly attachments and achieving divine realization through the practice of Dharma.

युधिष्ठिरःमनुदेहेन अमरः मर्त्येषु अभवत् |
पृथिविः स्वर्गभुता तद् मन्वन्तरौ अयं संपूर्णः ||71||

Yudhishthira, embodying all humanity, became immortal in a mortal body. Earth became a heaven, completing this cycle of creation (manvantara).
This verse portrays Yudhishthira as a symbol of human potential, achieving immortality within a mortal

body. His attainment of immortality signifies the highest spiritual realization, where one transcends the limitations of life and death. Through his ascension, Earth itself becomes a heavenly realm, reflecting the transformation of consciousness within humanity.

This transition marks the culmination of a cosmic cycle or manvantara, where Earth, through the fulfillment of Dharma, evolves into a higher plane of existence. It symbolizes humanity's potential for enlightenment and the transformation of the world through the practice of truth and righteousness.

वेदस्य सारं भारतं भारतस्य अपि सा गीता |
गीता सा कृष्णकृष्णा कृष्णा गीता सप्तशतिः ||72||

The essence of the Vedas is the Mahabharata, and the essence of the Mahabharata is the Gita. There are two versions of the Gita: one by Krishna and one by Durga, known as the Saptashati.
This verse emphasizes that the teachings of the Mahabharata encapsulate the wisdom of the Vedas, with the Gita serving as its distilled essence. The Gita offers two paths to divine wisdom: Krishna's guidance to Arjuna and Durga's counsel as the Saptashati (the seven-hundred-verse text dedicated to the goddess). Both versions offer complementary insights into the path of Dharma and the realization of one's divine nature.

The Gita by Krishna provides the path of karma and devotion, while Durga's Saptashati represents the divine feminine aspect, focusing on the empowerment of inner strength and wisdom. Together, they present a holistic vision of spiritual evolution and the attainment of harmony within the self and the universe.

Phalashruti / Outcome of reciting these 72 verses

धर्मक्षेत्रे वर्तमाने युद्धे कृष्णे समुपस्थिते
पाठकाः अस्याः सप्ततयः भवन्ति अजरामराः

In this land of Dharma, at the present time, with Krishna's presence, those who understand these seventy verses have the opportunity to become immortal gods. This verse speaks to the transformative potential of understanding and embodying the teachings of the seventy verses. The "land of Dharma" refers to the earth, where life is a continual struggle to uphold truth and righteousness. With Krishna's guidance, those who internalize the essence of these verses achieve a divine state, symbolized as immortality.
The verse implies that true understanding leads to transcendence, where individuals can attain spiritual immortality by realizing their divine nature. This is the ultimate goal of Dharma and the teachings imparted by Krishna, guiding humanity toward godhood and liberation from the cycle of birth and death.

Epilogue

The verses shared above weave a profound tapestry of cosmic principles, drawing on the wisdom of the Mahabharata, Vedic philosophy, and Hindu cosmology. At the heart of these teachings lies an exploration of Dharma, karma, and the eternal struggle between light and darkness. They are not simply philosophical statements but serve as guidelines for understanding the self, society, and the universe, resonating as timeless truths applicable to every age.

The story of the Mahabharata is itself a microcosm of the cosmic play, with its diverse characters representing archetypes, cosmic forces, and the eternal dualities inherent in existence. Draupadi, an incarnation of Durga and a symbol of the earth, embodies the divine feminine power, aligning her destiny with the forces of Dharma. Her trials signify the plight and perseverance of the Earth and feminine energy under the forces of material desire, ignorance, and misuse. She is simultaneously Earth, wisdom, purity, and strength. Her relationship with the Pandavas and her encounters with darker forces reflect the necessity of balancing the forces of light and shadow to maintain cosmic harmony.

The concept of karma and Naishkarmya yoga (action without attachment) emerge as central teachings. Krishna's guidance to Arjuna on the battlefield encourages selflessness and detachment, emphasizing that true mastery lies in surrendering one's actions to the divine. This detachment is not about abstaining from action but rather transforming action into an offering to the supreme. When the individual ego dissolves, and actions are seen as expressions of divine will, one transcends the cycle of karma. Through such selfless action, one can navigate life's trials, maintaining inner peace and purpose.

An essential theme running through these verses is the idea of divine possession and inspiration. True action, free from karmic bondage, occurs when the individual is "possessed" by a deity or higher consciousness, as the verses state. This concept suggests that when one surrenders personal desires and allows a higher force to act through them, they achieve alignment with cosmic order. The spiritual path thus calls for a dissolution of the ego, a willingness to serve as a vessel for divine will, which ultimately liberates one from attachment and suffering.

The interplay of Devas and Asuras, Nagas and Garudas, Kauravas and Pandavas in these verses illustrates the duality inherent in creation. Each represents opposing cosmic forces—light and dark, stasis and change, purity and material desire. These opposing energies are neither good nor evil in an absolute sense; rather, they are essential aspects of the cosmic balance, fueling the dynamic process of evolution. Through their interactions, they maintain the wheel of time (kala chakra), driving the progression of all beings toward enlightenment. The victory over Draupadi, as a symbol of Earth's sovereignty, becomes the ultimate goal, attainable only by those who align with Dharma.

The verses also reflect on Swabhava (one's inherent nature) and Swadharma (one's duty based on nature). Each individual is composed of a unique blend of qualities (gunas) and societal archetypes (varnas), creating distinct roles within the cosmic order. Recognizing and embracing one's swabhava is essential to fulfilling one's role in life. The alignment with swadharma, or acting in accordance with one's true nature, is seen as the pathway to peace, harmony, and spiritual progress. By accepting one's role in society and acting without comparison or desire for another's path, one moves toward self-realization.

Draupadi's choice of the Pandavas signifies a deeper truth—the soul's alignment with righteous values. Her vow, which states that only one who can match her strength and humiliate her pride will be her lord, signifies the divine feminine's demand for an equal partnership. This choice signifies that spiritual union is not achieved through force but through balance, respect, and shared purpose. Draupadi's abduction by the Nagas symbolizes the forces of ignorance and desire that seek to dominate the divine feminine but are ultimately destined to fail in their pursuit of controlling spiritual wisdom.

Finally, these teachings underscore that true immortality lies not in the body but in aligning with Dharma and realizing one's divine nature. The cycle of creation, preservation, and destruction repeats endlessly, yet those who understand and embody these teachings transcend the limitations of life and death. The promise of immortality is extended to those who grasp the essence of the teachings, particularly in Krishna's Gita and Durga's Saptashati. By understanding the universal principles, one attains freedom from the cyclical nature of karma, achieving a state of divine consciousness.

In conclusion, the verses lead us to a profound realization: the purpose of life is not to conquer the world but to conquer oneself. By embracing our swabhava, surrendering personal desires, and acting as instruments of the divine, we align ourselves with the cosmic order. The teachings of the Mahabharata, the Gita, and the Saptashati serve as timeless guides, offering a pathway to inner peace, spiritual growth, and ultimate liberation. The journey is one of self-discovery, as each individual, like Arjuna, must confront their inner doubts, embrace their unique path, and realize the divine within. The eternal dance of Devas and Asuras, Nagas and Garudas, plays on, with each soul participating in the unfolding of cosmic harmony. The true victory lies not in the outer world but in the inner realization of unity with the divine